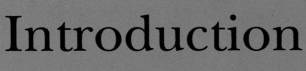

Introduction

Have you ever looked
up into the dark sky at
night and wondered
what is out there?

This book will take you out on
a fantastic journey of space
exploration to the outer limits
of the Universe.

Find out how scientists explore
space with the use of telescopes,
satellites, rockets and much
more. Learn about probes that
have been sent to explore far
away planets and find out
whether scientists have
found life on other planets.

Spot and count!

Q: Why watch out for these boxes?

A: They give answers to the space questions you always wanted to ask.

zoom in on...

Space bits

Look out for these
boxes to take a closer
look at space features.

Awesome factS

Watch out for these diamonds to learn more
about the truly weird and wonderful facts
about space and journeys of space
exploration.

Exploring space

In July 1969 American astronauts set foot on the Moon. It was the first time humans had ever stepped onto another world. Since then scientists have probed further and further into space. Using telescopes, robot probes, rockets and satellites, they have explored moons, planets, stars, galaxies and beyond.

Astronomers use powerful telescopes to study the night sky. As telescopes become more and more powerful, astronomers can see millions of previously unseen stars and galaxies. Telescopes in space have even captured images of galaxies millions of light years away.

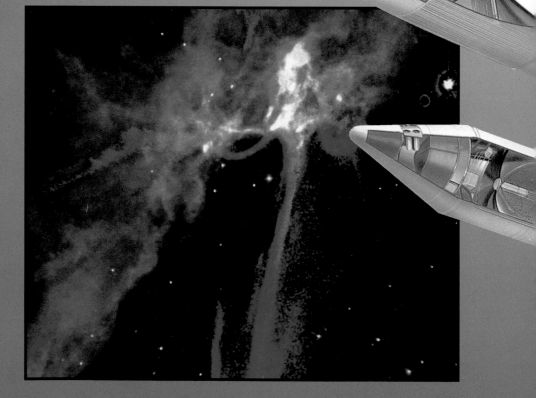

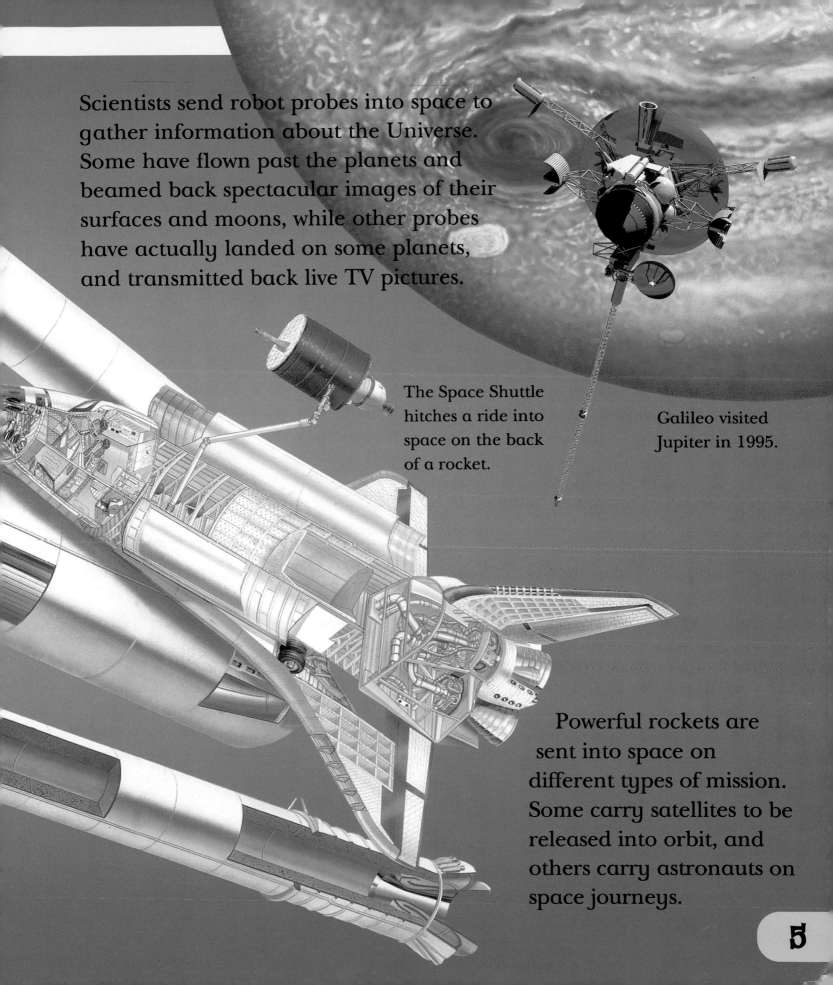

Scientists send robot probes into space to gather information about the Universe. Some have flown past the planets and beamed back spectacular images of their surfaces and moons, while other probes have actually landed on some planets, and transmitted back live TV pictures.

The Space Shuttle hitches a ride into space on the back of a rocket.

Galileo visited Jupiter in 1995.

Powerful rockets are sent into space on different types of mission. Some carry satellites to be released into orbit, and others carry astronauts on space journeys.

Observatories

Astronomers study the stars from buildings called observatories. These are often built on mountaintops away from low clouds and city lights to give a clear view of the night sky.

Awesome factS

The world's largest observatory is 4,200 m high, near the top of Mauna Kea in Hawaii.

Observatory

An observatory is a building that houses a telescope. Most have a domed roof which rotates with the telescope during the night so that it can keep aiming at the same stars as the Earth rotates.

Telescopes

Telescopes give a bigger or brighter view of distant objects. Some telescopes use lenses, others use mirrors.

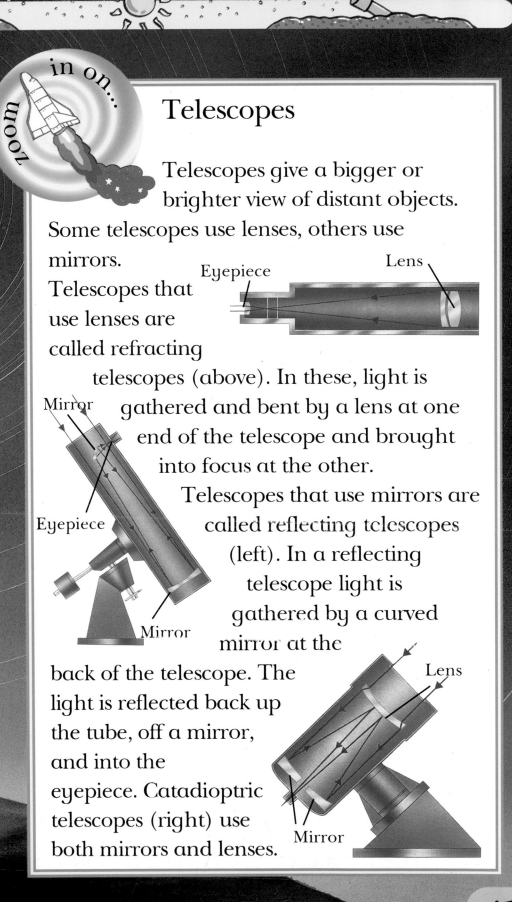

Eyepiece

Lens

Telescopes that use lenses are called refracting telescopes (above). In these, light is gathered and bent by a lens at one end of the telescope and brought into focus at the other.

Mirror

Eyepiece

Mirror

Telescopes that use mirrors are called reflecting telescopes (left). In a reflecting telescope light is gathered by a curved mirror at the back of the telescope. The light is reflected back up the tube, off a mirror, and into the eyepiece. Catadioptric telescopes (right) use both mirrors and lenses.

Lens

Mirror

7

Space telescopes

Not only does a position in orbit offer a good view of space, without the obstruction of the Earth's atmosphere, it also offers a good view of Earth. For these reasons astronomers are sending more and more telescopes into space to get the best possible views.

Q: How did Hubble get into space?

A: The Hubble Space Telescope was carried into space by the Space Shuttle. It was unloaded in space by the shuttle astronauts and sent into orbit. It is still beaming back amazing pictures to us from space.

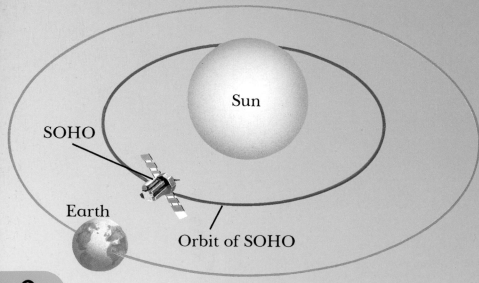

SOHO (the Solar and Heliospheric Observatory) was designed to study the Sun and was launched into orbit between the Earth and the Sun. Among other things SOHO has studied the Sun's insides and sunspots on the Sun's surface.

Sun

SOHO

Earth

Orbit of SOHO

The most famous of the space telescopes now orbiting around the Earth is the Hubble Space Telescope (HST), launched in 1990. The HST has a reflecting telescope which can see five times more detail than any ground-based telescope.

The world's biggest single radio telescope dish is the Arecibo telescope in Puerto Rico. It is a vast, smooth concrete dish 305 m across. Such a huge dish can pick up even very faint radio signals from space and listen for signs of life far out in the Universe.

How many dishes can you see?

Radio telescopes

We can see the visible light that stars give off, but they also give off other rays, such as radio waves and X-rays which our eyes cannot detect. Radio telescopes are able to pick up radio rays from a long distance.

Radio telescopes look like huge TV satellite dishes. They pick up radio signals from space. Because radio waves are much longer than light waves, radio telescope dishes have to be much, much bigger than ordinary telescopes. Many are more than 100 m across. Several smaller radio telescopes can be linked so that they work as a single, large telescope.

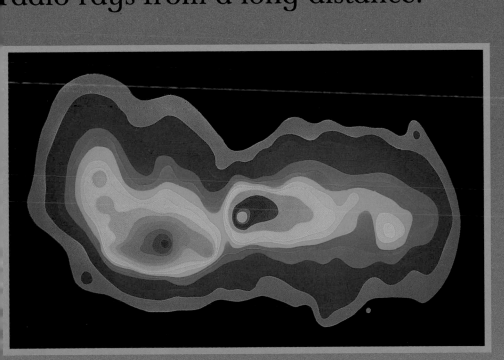

Rockets

Escaping the pull of the Earth's gravity demands enormous power. Special engines called rockets are used to get a spacecraft to a speed great enough to blast clear of Earth.

Command module

Satellite released into orbit.

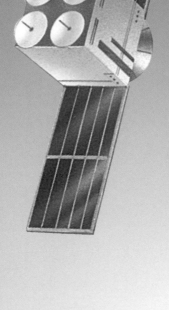

Service module

Apollo lunar module

Rockets need an enormous amount of fuel to get into orbit. They are basically giant fuel tanks. The Saturn V, which carried the Apollo spacecraft and astronauts to the Moon, was over 110 m tall. The command, service and lunar modules sat on top of three stages. When one stage was exhausted, it fell away and the next rocket stage took over.

USA

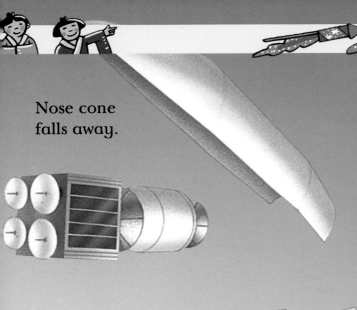

Nose cone falls away.

Spacecraft are usually boosted into space by powerful 'launch vehicles' which provide the power for the take-off thrust. These are rockets in three or four parts or stages. Each stage is designed to fall away once the craft has reached a certain height or speed.

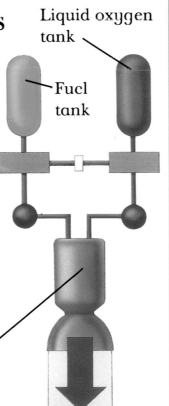

Third stage

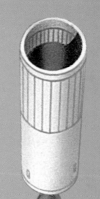

Second stage

First stage boosters fall away.

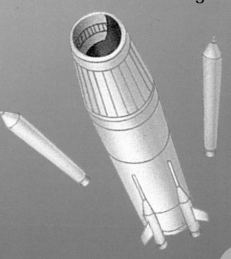

Rocket engines

Most big rockets are powered by liquid fuels. In order to burn, the fuel needs oxygen, so rockets also carry a supply of liquid oxygen as well as the fuel they need. The fuel and oxygen mix in a combustion chamber and burn with explosive force, driving the spacecraft forwards.

Liquid oxygen tank

Fuel tank

Combustion chamber

Once in space the craft needs much less fuel and smaller rockets which manoeuvre and steer in different directions. The spacecraft that continues on the journey after all the launch rockets have fallen away is usually tiny — typically less than a tenth of the size it was on the ground.

Astronauts orbiting the Earth are weightless. They can float around the cabin from one place to another. To sleep they must fasten themselves to their bed, or they will float away in the night.

Space flights

Once a spacecraft has escaped the Earth's gravity, it can travel huge distances using very little power. It uses small booster rockets, which help it to steer and give it a push in the right direction.

Q: What is escape velocity?

A: Satellites circle around the Earth, but they don't fly off into space because they are held in orbit by the Earth's strong gravity. Spacecraft can only break free of the Earth's gravity and venture out into space if they can reach a speed of 40,000 km/h. This is called escape velocity. If a craft reaches a somewhat lower speed, it goes into orbit around Earth, held there by the Earth's strong gravity.

The Shuttle blasts off with five engines. Two booster engines and the main fuel tank fall away in stages. When its mission is finished, it corrects its path and re-enters the Earth's atmosphere. It then glides back to Earth, landing like an aeroplane.

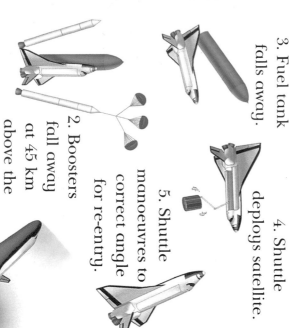

1. Launch

2. Boosters fall away at 45 km above the ground.

3. Fuel tank falls away.

4. Shuttle deploys satellite.

5. Shuttle manoeuvres to correct angle for re-entry.

6. Re-entry

7. Shuttle glides back to Earth so it can be re-used.

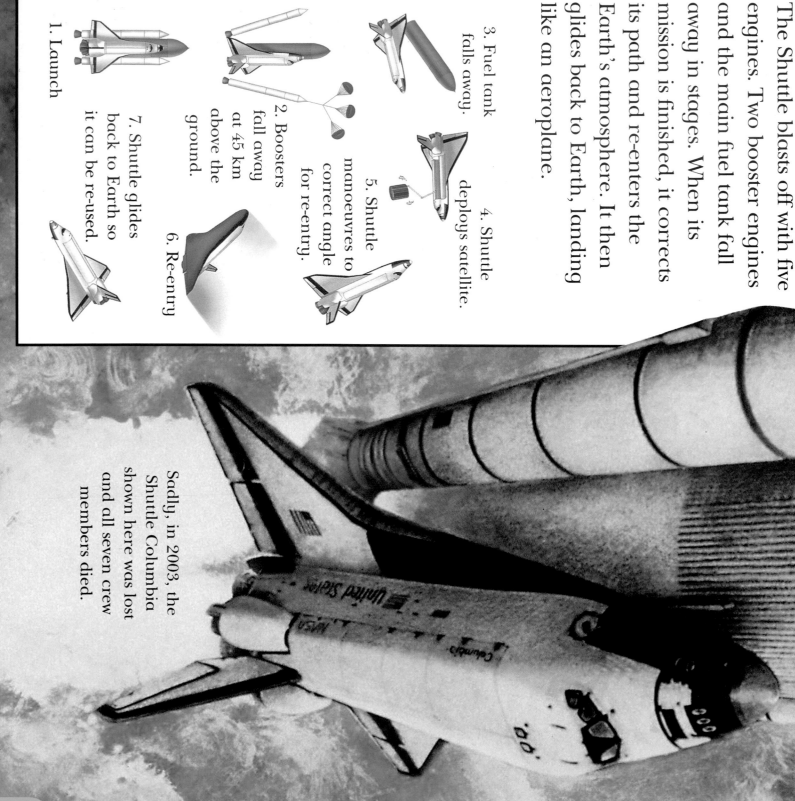

Sadly, in 2003, the Shuttle Columbia shown here was lost and all seven crew members died.

Space Shuttle

The Space Shuttle is a unique spacecraft because it can be launched again and again. It can ferry scientists to space laboratories, launch small satellites, or carry crews to repair satellites already in orbit.

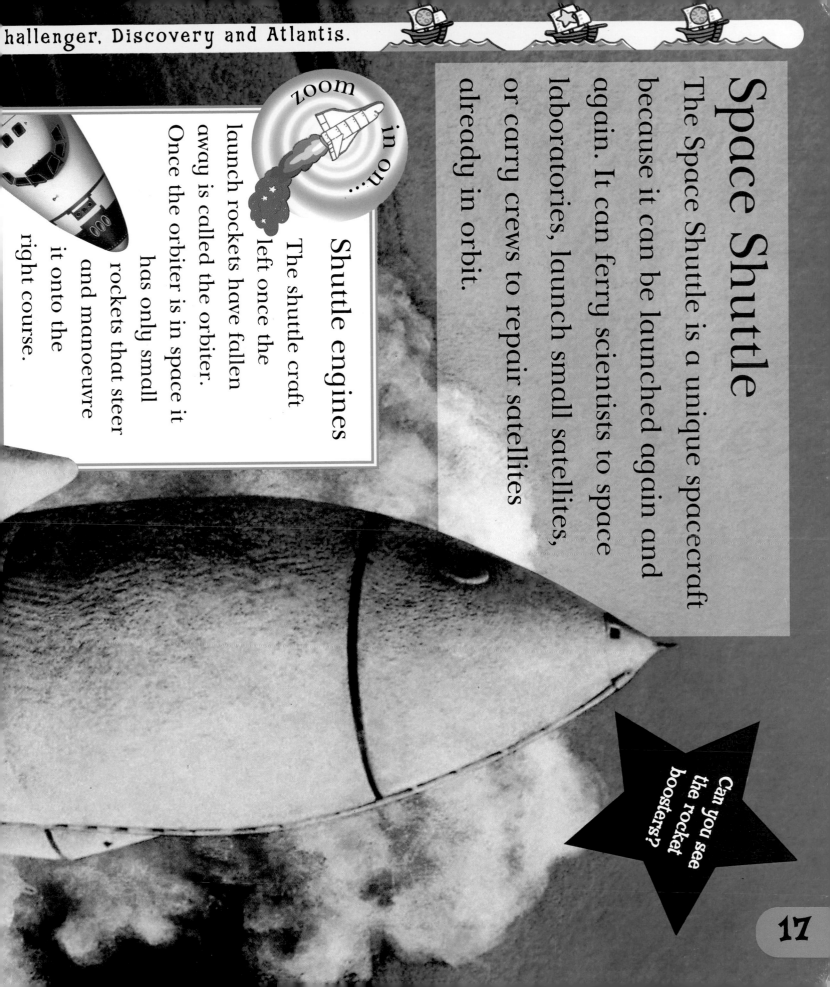

zoom in on...

Shuttle engines

The shuttle craft left once the launch rockets have fallen away is called the orbiter. Once the orbiter is in space it has only small rockets that steer and manoeuvre it onto the right course.

Can you see the rocket boosters?

17

Many satellites are used for communication, transmitting anything from television pictures to internet data. Live TV pictures can be transmitted all over the world. They are beamed up to a satellite high above the Earth, bounced on to another and beamed back down to Earth again instantly.

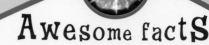

Awesome factS

There have now been over 5,000 satellites in space. Many of them are now useless bits of space junk.

Shuttle can communicate directly with Earth.

When shuttle is out of sight, signals can be bounced off a relay satellite.

Signals can be received almost instantly thousands of kilometres away.

Most satellites go only into relatively low orbits. Some are placed in space by the Space Shuttle. Shuttle astronauts can also carry out repairs on these low-orbiting satellites.

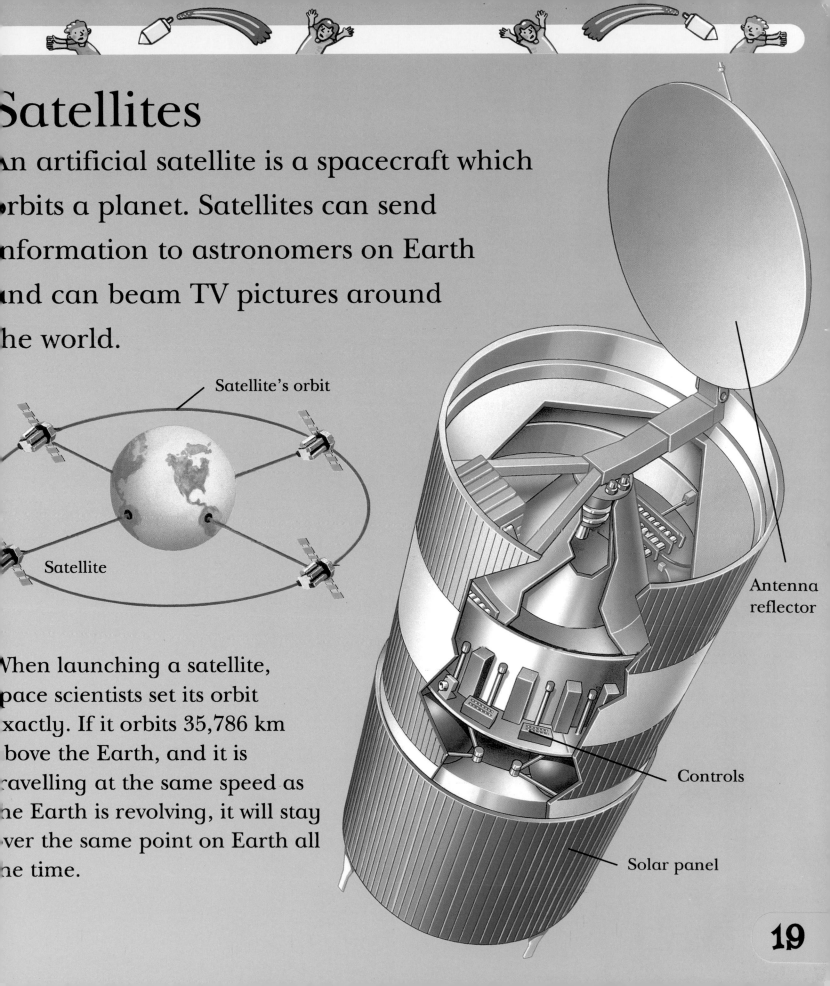

Satellites

An artificial satellite is a spacecraft which orbits a planet. Satellites can send information to astronomers on Earth and can beam TV pictures around the world.

Satellite's orbit

Satellite

When launching a satellite, space scientists set its orbit exactly. If it orbits 35,786 km above the Earth, and it is travelling at the same speed as the Earth is revolving, it will stay over the same point on Earth all the time.

Antenna reflector

Controls

Solar panel

Astronauts

Training for space missions is long and tough. Astronauts must be able to handle many kinds of equipment. They must also be healthy and strong to cope with weightlessness and spacewalks.

zoom in on...

Growing in space

When you sleep, gravity stops pressing your back bones together, so you are a little taller in the morning. The same thing happens to astronauts in space, where gravity doesn't press at all.

Weightlessness makes astronauts feel sick until they get used to it. Before going into space, they train underwater or in aeroplanes that are diving towards the Earth, to learn how to work in weightlessness.

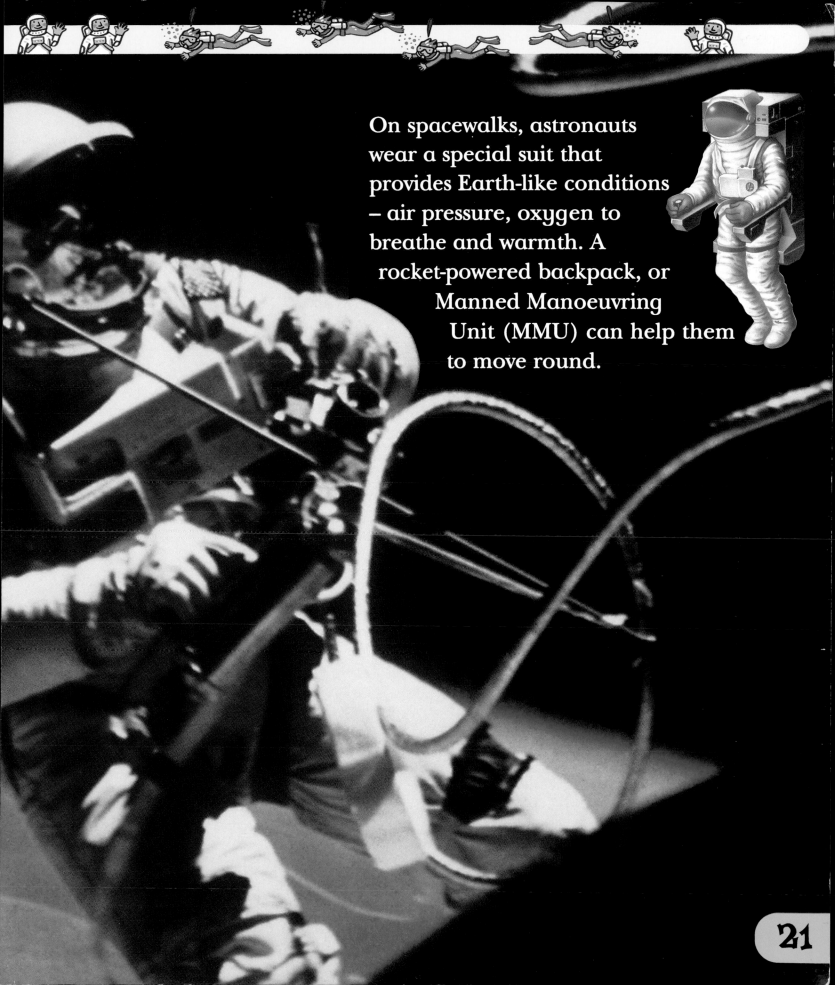

On spacewalks, astronauts
wear a special suit that
provides Earth-like conditions
– air pressure, oxygen to
breathe and warmth. A
rocket-powered backpack, or
Manned Manoeuvring
Unit (MMU) can help them
to move round.

Q: What was Skylab made of?

A: Skylab was made from the third-stage casing of the Saturn V rocket. Launched in 1973, it was in orbit for six years. When it re-entered the atmosphere, parts that didn't burn up landed in Australia.

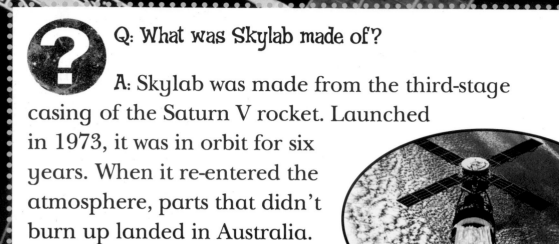

zoom in on...

Living in space

The crew of a space station has to get used to living in weightless conditions. Even simple things, that we on Earth take for granted, must be planned carefully. Food and drink are taken from pouches. Otherwise they would float off plates and out of glasses. Astronauts also need exercise so spacecraft are fitted with special exercise equipment.

Space stations

The International Space Station (ISS) is a huge space station that is being built in space. It will be as big as two jumbo jets when it is finished and it will be used for experiments in space. A crew of up to six people will live on board.

Can you see the solar panels which provide energy?

23

Mercury has been visited only by Mariner 10, which flew past it three times in 1974 and 1975. It got to within 300 km of the surface but was able to map less than half of the planet. It found that Mercury's surface is much like the surface of the Moon, covered in rocky craters thought to be from impacts millions of years ago.

zoom in on...

Mars visit

A recent Mars mission was the American Mars Pathfinder expedition which landed on 4th July 1997. Pathfinder bounced onto Mars's surface, protected by airbags. The probe then released a small robot vehicle called Sojourner which could be controlled from Earth. It was used to explore the Martian landscape.

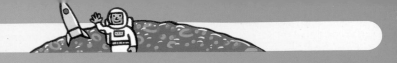

Visiting the inner planets

Mercury and Venus are difficult to observe from Earth. Mercury is very close to the Sun, and Venus is covered in thick clouds of gas. The only details of these planets have been supplied by probes. Mars is easier to explore and is the most visited of all the planets.

Can you see the space probe Venera?

Many missions have flown past Venus. A few have succeeded in landing on the planet's surface to send back data about its harsh conditions. In 1990, the U.S. Magellan probe peered through the thick clouds of Venus's atmosphere to map the planet's surface by radar. It found mountains and volcanoes up to eight km high.

Venera

Visiting the outer planets

Voyages to the outer planets – Jupiter, Saturn, Uranus, Neptune and Pluto – are much harder. The distances are huge, which means radio communications take several hours, and the probes must pass through hazardous radiation belts near Jupiter if they journey out that far.

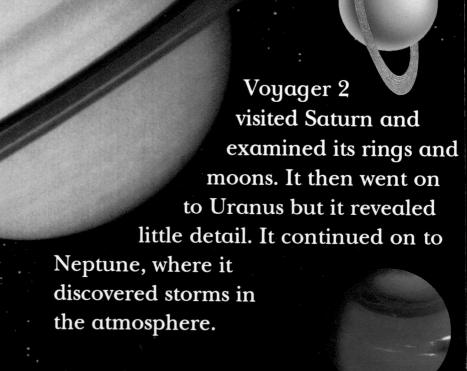

Voyager

Voyager 2 visited Saturn and examined its rings and moons. It then went on to Uranus but it revealed little detail. It continued on to Neptune, where it discovered storms in the atmosphere.

Jupiter was first visited by the American Pioneer 10 probe in 1973. Pioneer 11 first reached Saturn in 1979. The first good images of these planets came from Voyager probes in 1979-81. They took close-ups of Jupiter's moons and surface and showed that Io, one of Jupiter's moons, had active volcanoes on its surface.

Pioneer

The Pioneer and Voyager probes went to the outer planets of the Solar System using the sling-shot effect. Each spacecraft flew close to a planet and used the planet's speed around the Sun to propel it further out into the Solar System.

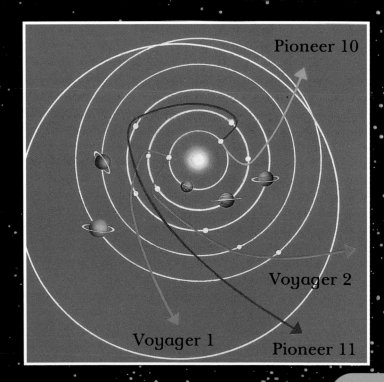

Pioneer 10

Voyager 2

Voyager 1

Pioneer 11

Future missions

The future holds many new and exciting developments in space exploration. One project, VentureStar, is planned as a replacement for the Space Shuttle and is designed to be a light single-stage launch vehicle. It would be a lot cheaper to run, costing one tenth of a shuttle flight.

Mars Direct is a plan to send a robot factory to Mars to make fuel from Mars's atmosphere for a return journey. A second ship would follow later, carrying humans. They would use the fuel for a return flight to Earth.

It would be possible to propel a craft away from the Sun by using the solar wind, a stream of particles which flows from the star. Such a craft would use a huge sail to capture the power of the solar wind and propel it out into space. The sail could fold away once the effects of the solar wind were no longer felt.

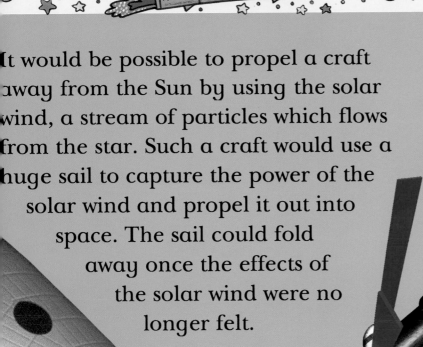

Space is so huge that travel can take a long time. For this reason, scientists have designed a huge space ark where astronauts could grow their own food, or even rear animals on a long journey.

 Q: Will there be day trips to the Moon?

A: At the moment a trip to the Moon would take longer than one day but advances in technology means that space travel is becoming faster.

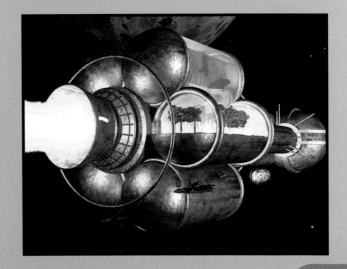

Space missions

There have been so many missions into space that it is difficult to remember all of them. However here are some of the most recent missions and even some more planned for the future!

Mars Direct

A mission to Mars would cost billions of dollars. A cheaper alternative planned is Mars Direct. A robot factory would be sent to Mars where it would create fuel for a return journey cutting the cost of any mission by a huge amount.

Mars Surveyor

The Mars Global Surveyor reached Mars in September 1997. Its mission is to accurately map the planet's entire surface. From its orbit around Mars, its cameras can see objects that are less than one metre across.

Cassini

Cassini will reach Saturn in 2004 and will spend four years in orbit looking at the planet. It also carries a small probe called Huygens which it will drop onto Saturn's moon, Titan.

IRAS

The IRAS satellite was designed to pick up radiation given out by anything hot. IRAS turned gradually round to map a picture of the entire sky. It picked up asteroids, comet dust trails and gas and dust where stars were being born.

Glossary

Astronauts
People who travel into space. Russian astronauts are called cosmonauts.

Atmosphere
The layer of gases that surrounds a planet.

Black hole
The remains of a huge star that has exploded. The gravity is so strong that not even light can escape.

Escape velocity
The speed at which a rocket has to travel in order to escape from the pull of the Earth's gravity. Escape velocity is 40,000 km/h.

Gravity
Every object in the Universe has a force that attracts it to every other object. This force is called gravity. The Solar System is held together by the Sun's gravitational pull.

Observatory
A building that houses a telescope.

Orbit
The path of one object around another object.

Orbiter
An artificial satellite after the launch rockets and boosters have fallen away.

Probe
An unmanned spacecraft sent from Earth to explore an object in space.

Radiation
Energy that can be visible light, or waves that our eyes cannot see, such as X-rays or radio waves.

Rockets
Powerful motors that produce thrust to blast off into space.

Satellite
An object that orbits another larger object. Satellites can be natural such as moons, or artificial such as a spacecraft.

Solar panels
Panels on a spacecraft that convert the Sun's light into energy for power.

Solar wind
A stream of particles that flows from the Sun.

Stages
Rockets may come in parts, called stages. Each stage contains its own rocket motors and fuel.

Telescope
An instrument that collects light and radiation and magnifies them to help astronomers to study the sky.

X-rays
Radiation that cannot be seen with the naked eye.

Index

Photocredits
Abbreviations: t-top, m-middle, b-bottom, r-right, l-left, c-centre
Cover, 3tl, 4bl, 9, 16-17, 18mr, 20-21, 22t, 24m, 26c, 26mr, 26br – Corbis.
10tr – Roger Ressmeyer/CORBIS. 11ml – B. Cooper & D. Parker/Science
Photo Library. 12bl, 15tr, 25 br both, 27tl, 28tl, 31tl – Stockbyte. 14ml,
22-23 – CORBIS. 14m – Bettmann/CORBIS. 28tr – NASA.